Library of Congress Control Number: 2010939244

ISBN 978-1-58150-341-8

Printed in the United States
First Edition: 2010

EP
ECLIPSE
PRESS

a division of
Blood-Horse Publications
PUBLISHERS SINCE 1916

Primerica

JANE LYON AND KAREN BAILEY

ILLUSTRATIONS BY SUSIE GORDON

"Ah, there was a time,"
He was heard to say
As he nibbled the last
Of his stemmy hay.

"Oh! Not that again!"
His stablemate said,
With a roll of his eyes
And a shake of his head.

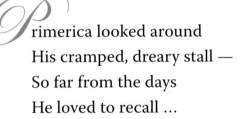

Primerica looked around
His cramped, dreary stall —
So far from the days
He loved to recall …

Born in Kentucky
With blue blood in his veins,
He had run at great racetracks,
The best jocks at his reins.

He, his sister, and brother
Had won stakes at the game,
And he always was proud
To stand up for his name.

$\mathcal{H}$e believed that no matter
What level the test
That honor demanded
You give it your best!

But of all of his memories he loved most to recall
Was the "Great Grade I" race
That he ran in the fall.

"Let's see … was it '03
or was it '04?
It's funny, but it's hard
to remember for sure."

The sun shone down as we stepped on the track ….
The crowd went wild when the jockeys got on our backs.

One by one, they led us into the gates.
Seconds seemed forever as we awaited our fates …

Great Grade1

12

"In case you don't know," he said to his friend,
"Grade I is the best class you can ever run in!"

"Yeah, yeah, I know," the old gray said,
"So how'd you get from the top to the bottom instead?"

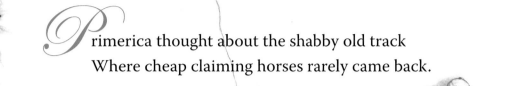

Primerica thought about the shabby old track
Where cheap claiming horses rarely came back.

"My bones do ache, and my hooves get sore,
But I'm ten after all; I'm not young anymore."

Susie Tendon

"I don't really know where my siblings have gone;
I heard Mom went to Kentucky —
But that's been so long …

When you can't win a stakes race, they drop to allowance
Then down to claiming to even the balance.

There are so many horses with nowhere to go.
Some just keep on running 'til they can't run anymore."

ut you still have to try
No matter the test
Because honor demands
You give it your best!"

"Well, my race is today," Primerica said to his friend. "So I'll give it my best ... Hey! I might even win!"

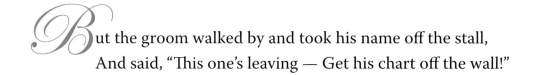

But the groom walked by and took his name off the stall,
And said, "This one's leaving — Get his chart off the wall!"

Terror shot through his heart; his eyes started to burn.
Was it the "stockyard van" where you never return?

STOCKYARDS

NO OUTLET
DEAD END

ONE
WAY

Though he knew it might mean his last ride was near
He held his head high and showed them no fear.

His body was shaking as they led him away
Then they bedded him down …
In knee-deep hay!

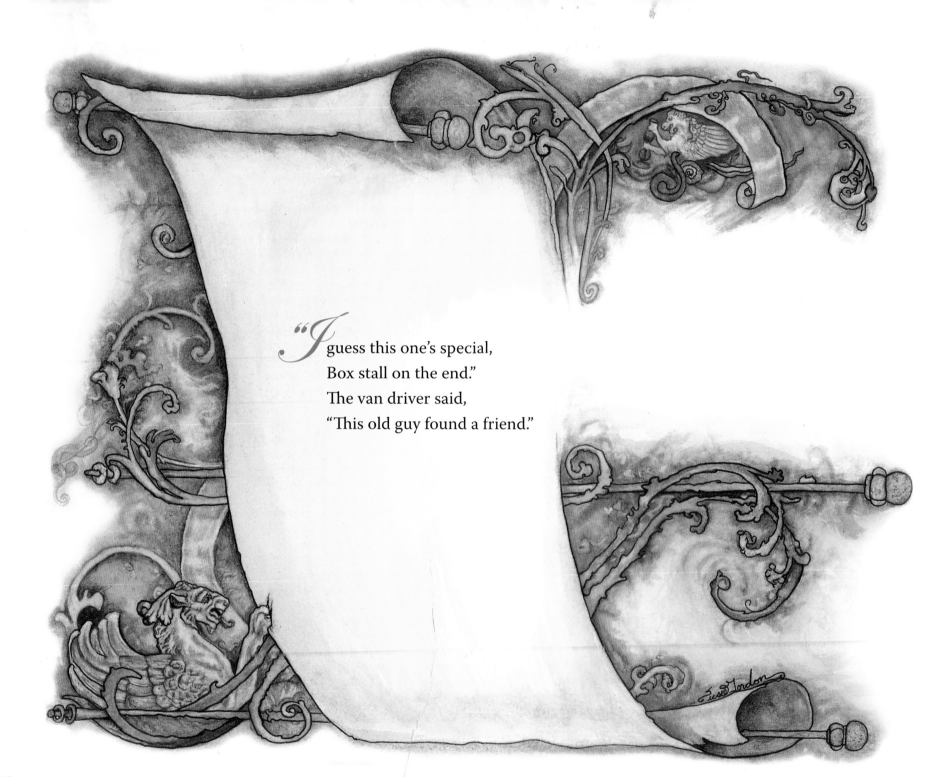

"I guess this one's special,
Box stall on the end."
The van driver said,
"This old guy found a friend."

26

Where am I going?
What's this about?
Primerica wondered …
He guessed he'd find out!

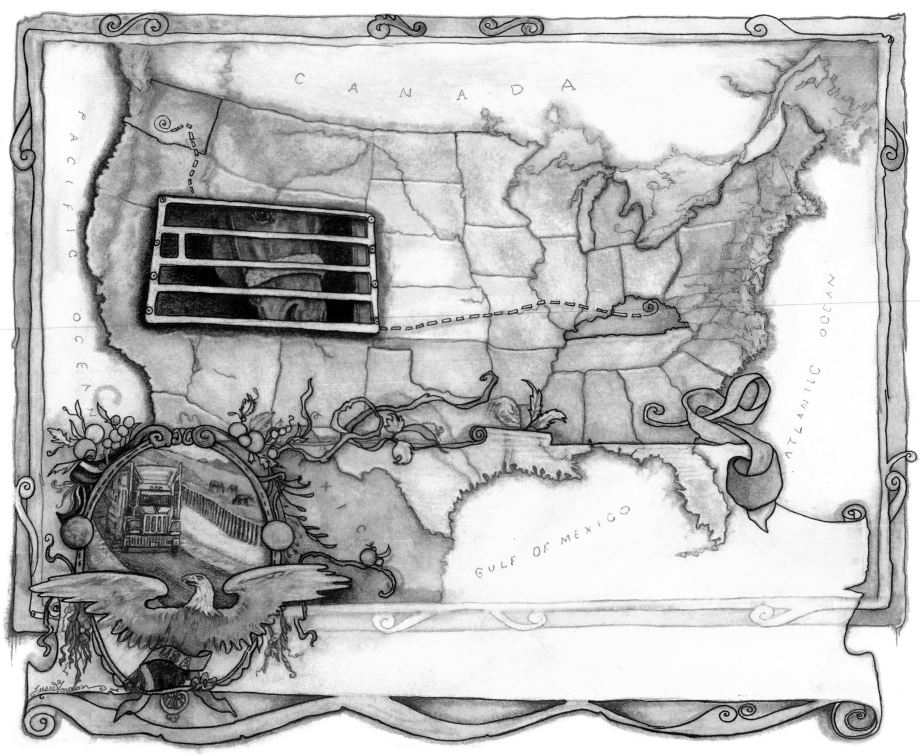

Many hours later, from Washington state,
The van pulled up to the Kentucky farm's gate!

There to meet him together
With tears in their eyes
Were the owners and his mother
Under Summer Wind skies.

All along they'd been searching
And following his path,
So when it was time,
He would come home at last!

EPILOGUE

Primerica often thinks about his old friend and wonders whatever happened to him. He hopes there are others willing to save a place in their hearts … and a home for the brave.

PRIMERICA'S STORY

PRIMERICA logged many miles and passed through many hands during his years on the racetrack. Bred in Kentucky by Irwin and France Weiner, the son of Mr. Greeley—Primedex was born on February 15, 1998. He sold for $280,000 at the 2000 Fasig-Tipton Florida select 2-year-olds in training sale after failing to sell as a yearling.

Primerica didn't make it to the races until age 4, racing for the Jess L. Miller Trust in Southern California. In his first start, on January 19, 2002, at Santa Anita Park, Primerica finished third. He won by five lengths next time out under jockey Patrick Valenzuela, who would partner with him many times. In 2003 Primerica raced in the grade I Triple Bend Breeders' Cup Invitational Handicap and was placed third. The Triple Bend was the most prestigious race in which Primerica would compete. Soon after, he was claimed for the first of many

times; he would sell for less and less each time.

In all, Primerica raced 38 times, winning eight times and earning nearly $400,000.

As Primerica reached age 9, though, he did not show the same competitiveness. He began racing in $10,000 claiming races and finished ninth in his last start, December 9, 2007, at Hollywood Park. By then, his waning career had come to the attention of Jane Lyon, owner of Summer Wind Farm in Kentucky. Mrs. Lyon had purchased the dam, Primedex, and kept track of horses to which the farm had a connection. "He came up in my virtual stable, and I realized he was getting pretty old and was in pretty bad circumstances, so I bought him back," she said.

Primerica arrived at Summer Wind "in pretty bad shape" but underwent a successful recuperation and today enjoys life as a beloved "pasture ornament."

Jane Lyon with Primerica and Karen Bailey
with Skipingo at Summer Wind Farm

KAREN BAILEY

JANE LYON *AND*

JANE LYON is living her lifelong dream of raising Thoroughbreds in the bluegrass of Kentucky. An avid animal lover, she and her daughter **KAREN BAILEY** are intimately involved in every aspect of the family's Summer Wind Farm near Georgetown and are dedicated to equine welfare. Jane has written poetry

KAREN BAILEY

for years and is the co-author, with Karen, of *Skipingo Home*, a children's book about a horse they bred and brought home. Karen is an accomplished hunter-jumper rider and a licensed wildlife rehabilitator.

Proceeds from *Primerica* and *Skipingo Home* go to organizations that promote Thoroughbred rescue.

ANNE M. EBERHARDT

Susie Gordon

THE SOFT YET DETAILED DRAWINGS of Susie Gordon add a realistic touch to the children's books *Primerica* and *Skipingo Home* and the stories they tell about racehorses given second chances. Complete with a tint of color, the drawings subtly show how "things really look," according to Gordon.

Although children's book illustration is fairly new to Gordon, she is a longtime artist known for her love of animals, including the horse. She is a frequent exhibitor at the American Academy of Equine Art's fall show and exhibition.

Gordon was trained at the acclaimed Columbus College of Art and Design, where she worked in fine art painting and lost wax bronze, and at the Beartooth School of Art, where she trained with Carl Brenders. Her work, including the award-winning tiger painting, *Behold*, recently was offered to the public.

Gordon lives in North Lewisburg, Ohio, with her husband, Eric, and children, Tristan, Miriam, and Landon. Among the numerous animals she counts as family are Welsh Mountain ponies, Arabian horses, a Friesian mare, Scottish deerhounds, a border collie, and a schipperke.